MOTIVATING ILLUSTRATIONS OF FAITH IN BASKETBALL

by

Micheal L. Jones

"Motivating Illustrations of Faith in Basketball," by Micheal L. Jones.

ISBN 978-1-62137-514-2 (softcover).

Published 2013, 2014 by Virtualbookworm.com Publishing Inc., P.O. Box 9949, College Station, TX 77842, US. ©2013, Micheal L. Jones. All rights reserved. No part of this publication may be reproduced, stored in a retrieval system, or transmitted in any form or by any means, electronic, mechanical, recording or otherwise, without the prior written permission of Micheal L. Jones.

Manufactured in the United States of America.

Introduction

The game of basketball was birthed from James Naismith in 1891. He was given a task to develop an indoor game for when it was too cold for outdoor activities. So, while an employee of the YMCA, he created the world famous game called basketball.

He believed that this was a way to minister across the world. So now, I plan to take his philosophy and illustrate what he saw in essence as a concept to those that are in the athletic industry, to motivate you with concepts of the purpose of the game. The game of basketball was derived from 7 sports; rugby, lacrosse, soccer, football, hockey, and baseball. Once basketball was developed, then volleyball was developed by William Morgan, which was inspired by James Naismith. James Naismith was also a minister of God. However, he left the church to use basketball as ministry across the earth (Rains, 2009).

Acknowledgements

I would like to thank God, my family, and everyone who helps inspire me to become the best.

TABLE OF CONTENTS

HYPOTHESIS 1:

Hypothesis Illustration of Dr. Naismith's Vision with
Theology

James Naismith (Founder of Basketball/YMCA)

Rugby + Lacrosse + Soccer + Football + Hockey + Baseball
=
Basketball

William Morgan (Founder of Volleyball/YMCA)

Since William Morgan was inspired by basketball, he created the
game called mintonette (or volleyball).

Basketball birthed Volleyball.

Kevin Conner (Theologist)
Known for interpreting symbols and types in the Bible.
Volleyball is the 8th Sport.

Volleyball
=
New Beginnings

Based upon Hypothesis 1, you notice that each individual
that is mentioned is a Christian. So, if they are Christian, then the
possibility of them having Christian concepts in there creating
thinking could also be faith based. Therefore, I've interpreted a

concept of illustrative concepts of faith symbols in the sport of basketball.

According to Conner (Interpreting Symbols and Types, 1992), the number 8 represents new beginnings.) So, in understanding that volleyball was developed after basketball, this was the new creation based upon William Morgan's thought process of volleyball.

This book was designed to help motivate those in the athletic industry through faith. By interpreting symbols and types, the bible, and sports, this information can help you understand more about the game of basketball and its purpose. In reviewing the book *"James Naismith, The Man Who Invented Basketball by Rob Rains (2009)*), you can note that James Naismith believed in using basketball as a tool to change people's lives. He was a Christian and believed in biblical principles. The purpose of this researched concept is to visually show how basketball must be understood. This document does not replace the Bible; it is only used to help you understand basketball through faith. In using the original theory from*"The Basketball Dreamer of Branded Caliber Manual by Micheal Jones (2010),* additions have been made to help better understand the purpose of the manual. I hope everyone that reads this book will be motivated.

HYPOTHESIS 2:

Illustrations of Faith & Basketball Table

In order to understand the concept of this book, you will need to understand this hypothesis:
Church = Gym
Outer Court, Inner Court, Holy of Holys = Basketball Court
Priest = Basketball Coach
Provision = Basket
Word of God = Basketball
Elders = Basketball Officials
Five Fold Ministry = Starting 5 line up
Signs and Season = Scoreboard
Congregation Pews = Bleachers
Guards = Security
Tithes and Offering = Admission
The Arc = the 3pt Arc for Shooters
Fasting = Performance
Adversary = Opponents
Praise and Worship = Warm-ups
Ushers = Ushers
Nets = Catcher
10 Commandments = Basketball Rules
Soul Salvation = Training
Playing Basketball = Living Sacrifice
Plays = Study of Approval
Score Table = Altar

Illustration of Church

=

Gymnasium

"A Basketball Gymnasium is like a church or sanctuary."

Matthew 16: 18 (NIV)
And I tell you that you are Peter, and on this rock I will build my church and the gates of Hades will not overcome it.

In *"The Man Who Invented Basketball"* Raines (2009), the introduction paragraph on page 12 stated:
"[He] marveled at how popular basketball became in churches and as more and more churches built new gymnasiums, he was amazed and pleased.

In faith, understand the concept of church. Churches built gyms because of the work that was being done by James Naismith. Gym settings look almost like church settings. In faith, I believe that Mr. Naismith wanted someone to see God through basketball. Who saves the athlete, when the athlete does not go to church? The coach supposed to. Coaches, please get motivated to help save your athletes in all things, including their souls.

Illustration of Church Court
=
Basketball Court

"A basketball court is like the outer court, inner court, and
the Holy of Holys."
(Ex: out of bounds, in bounds, center court):

Out of bounds is like the outer court
In bounds is like the inner court
Center court is like the Holy of Holys

Psalms 100:4 (NIV)
*Enter His gates with thanksgiving and His courts with praise;
give thanks to Him and praise His name.*

This concept should be used to bless God just as if you were
at church. You use this to help you spiritually in preparing for the
game. Pregame warm-up is so important. This could help you
either have a good game or a bad game. Always prepare yourself.
The court is symbolic to motivate our memory for the great fight
in the end. (Reference Scripture): Jude 1:14-15.

ILLUSTRATION OF PRIEST

=

BASKETBALL COACH

"A basketball coach is like a Priest."

Exodus 19:6 (NIV)
*you will be for me a kingdom of priests and a holy nation. These
are words you are to speak to the Israelites.*

"Coaching and preaching are the same." We must remember
that in essence, James Naismith believed in helping others
through the game of basketball by passing the knowledge on to
others. We must pass on the gospel of basketball to others so that
they get the message.

ILLUSTRATION OF PROVISION

=

BASKET

"A basket is like provision for man."

Matthew 16:9 (NIV)
*Do you still not understand? Don't you remember the five loaves
for the five thousand and how many basketfuls you gathered?*

"Provision is something left for a purpose. According to
Conner (1992), a basket represents provision. I believe that
basketball was left and created for those that have a purpose in
expanding the vision, and to teach this game to change lives.
Naismith used a basket to help develop the game of basketball.
We should be motivated by the vision and provision that is left
for us. The basket gives us provision of what we as basketball
players should do. Fulfill the vision. The vision is to prepare for
spiritual warfare by playing basketball against an opponent.
There can only be one winner. In the bible, there is one winner.
So, in basketball, it can only be one winner.

Illustration of the Bible

=

Basketball

"A basketball is like the word of God."

John 1:14 (NIV)
The Word became flesh and made his dwelling among us. We have seen His glory, the glory of the One and only, who came from the Father, full of grace and truth.

Originally a basketball was made from strips of leather, so, something had to die in order for a basketball to be created. Likewise, Jesus had to die for us in order for us to live. If you dribbled a flat basketball, it would not bounce or make a sound. Why? The ball is dead, no air is present inside. Once air is pumped into the basketball, it is then useful. This is like God breathing inside of Adam, giving him life.

"If those that are chosen for basketball learn how to understand the Bible and basketball, they can motivate themselves into their purpose in life."

ILLUSTRATION OF ELDERS
=
BASKETBALL OFFICIALS

"A basketball official is like an elder clothed in authority."

1 Peter 2:25 (NIV)
For you were like sheep going astray, but now you have returned to the Shepherd and Overseer of your souls.

"If players get out of line, the official is there to correct them." Officials in basketball should be motivated by their position of authority. Most officials you see that referee basketball are older. In faith, you always want elders or referees with wisdom to oversee a game.

Illustration of Five Fold Ministry

=

Starting Five

"A starting 5 is like a representation of Five Fold Ministry."

Ephesians 4:11 (NIV)
It was He who gave some to be apostles, some to be prophets, some to be evangelists, and some to be pastors, and teachers.

A Point Guard is like an Apostle
(The leader with the basketball)

A Shooting Guard is like a Prophet
(The Archer)

A Small Forward is like an Evangelist
(The Roamer or Recruiter)

A Power Forward is like a Pastor
(The protector of the basket)

A Center is like a Teacher
(The protector of the basket with great Strength)

"The coach appoints his starting 5." Coaches, motivate yourselves to appoint your disciples to be the best at what they do.

Illustration of Signs and Seasons

=

Scoreboard

"The scoreboard is like signs and seasons."

2 Timothy 4:2 (NIV)
Preach the Word; be prepared in season; correct, rebuke and encourage with great patience and careful instruction.

"This concept is a reminder that time is always against us." Each quarter represents 25 years of our lives. We are blessed to get to 4th quarter. No matter the times in our lives, we must remember that there is a since of urgency to get the job done while we still have time. Winning is not everything, but we want to win at understanding the purpose. Even if we lose, we still win when we understand the message. Jesus took a loss by dying, so we all could win. Stay motivated, and do not leave the earth with your work undone.

ILLUSTRATION OF THE CONGREGATION

=

BLEACHERS

"Bleachers are like the congregation."

Psalms 26:12 (NIV)
My feet stand on level ground; in the great assembly
I will praise the Lord.

"The fans should always praise not only when someone wins, but praise God too." This is where everyone can participate in celebrating the purpose in God. Everyone, be motivated to give praise. Praise please people and God. Be motivated to give praise.

ILLUSTRATION OF GUARDS

=

SECURITY

"The security officer is like the guards of the church."

Ezekiel 44:16
They alone are to enter my sanctuary; they alone are to come near my table to minister before me and serve me as guards.

Police or security serve as your guards in the gym. Use this designated person as a guide for help and disputes in the gym. This keeps the gym safe of unwanted behavior. All Security guards, be motivated in your place of purpose to protect the house.

ILLUSTRATION OF TITHE AND OFFERINGS

=

GAME ADMISSIONS

"Admission fees are like tithes and offerings."

Malachi 3:8–9 (NIV)
Will a man rob God? Yet you rob me. But you ask, How do we rob you? In tithes and offerings. You are under a curse, the whole nation of you because you are robbing me.

Pay your admission fee when entering in any gym. This keeps the enemy away. Be glad about it. Also, be motivated to give more to support the purpose.

THE ARC

=

SHOOTERS OR JUMP SHOOTER (2 GUARDS)

"The Arc (3 point line) is like Archery for Shooters."

Genesis 21:20(NIV)
God was with the boy as he grew up. He lived in the desert and became an archer.

This illustration is mainly for 2 guards or shooting guards. You must be motivated to understand that from a great distance, you can make any shot only if you can believe.

FASTING

=

PERFORMANCE

"Fasting is like a diet regimen to help performance for the game of basketball."

Matthew 6:16
When you fast, do not look somber as the hypocrites do, for they disfigured their faces to show men they are fasting. I tell you the truth; they have received their reward in full.

Fasting is a lifestyle just like eating right and exercising. You will see results when your lifestyle changes in terms of your eating and workouts. Once this changes, then your performance increases. All, please remain motivated to fast to help peak performance.

ENEMY OR ADVERSARY

=

OPPONENTS

"The opposing basketball team is like the enemy."

John 10:10 (NIV)
The thief comes only to steal, kill, and destroy; I have come that they may have life, and have it to the full.

This concept lets you know that there is a counterfeit that is always against us. Spiritually, basketball is just a reminder of who we truly have to go against, which is the enemy. So, we must prepare every game like the other team is like the enemy. So when the day of judgment comes, we are ready to go up against the real enemy. This will be the game of all games. Be motivated to perform on this day like never before.

PRAISE AND WORSHIP

=

WARM-UP MUSIC

"Music is like praise and worship."

Psalms 100:4 (NIV)
Enter his gates with thanksgiving and his courts with praise; give thanks to him and praise his name.

Again, before the word comes, praise and worship must come forth. Music is a great motivation before the word comes forth. Music gets your spirit motivated to peak performance. Music is one of the most profound motivators to help basketball player perform. Coaches, what music do you allow your basketball players to listen too? Coaches, please make sure it's positive.

USHERS OR GATEKEEPERS
=
USHERS

"Ushers are like ushers seating you in church."

1 Chronicles 9:21
*Zechariah son of Meshelemiah was the **gatekeeper** at the entrance to the tent of meeting.*

This scripture gives reference to what users or gatekeepers are supposed to do. Ushers, be motivated to lead the people to their seat.

NETS
=
NETS

"The basketball nets are like the catcher for the basketball."

Matthew 4:18–19 (NIV)
As Jesus was walking beside the Sea of Galilee, he saw two brothers, Simon called Peter and his brother Andrew. They were casting a net into the lake, for they were fishermen. Come, follow me, Jesus said, and I will make you fishers of men.

Use the word of God to save others. The net is a reminder of you saving someone's life.

TEN COMMANDMENTS

=

BASKETBALL RULES

"Basketball rules are like the commandments."

Exodus 20:1—17 (NIV)
And God spoke all these words: I am the Lord your God, who brought you out of Egypt, out of the land of slavery. You shall have no other gods before me. You shall not make for yourself an idol in the form of anything in heaven above or on the earth beneath or in the waters below. You shall not bow down to them or worship them; for I, the Lord you God, am a jealous God, punishing the children for the sin of the fathers to the third and fourth generation of those who hate me, but showing love to a thousand generations of those who love me and keep my commandments. You shall not misuse the name of the Lord your God for the Lord will not hold anyone guiltless who misuses his name. Remember the Sabbath day by keeping it holy. Six days you shall labor and do all your work, but the seventh day is a Sabbath to the Lord your God. On it you shall not do any work, neither you, nor your son or daughter, nor your manservant or maidservant, nor your animals, nor the alien within your gates. For in six days the Lord made the heavens and the earth the sea, and all that is in them, but he rested on the seventh day. Therefore the Lord blessed the Sabbath day and made it holy.

Honor your father and your mother, so that you may live long in the land the Lord your God is giving you. You shall not murder.

You shall not commit adultery. You shall not steal. You shall not give false testimony against your neighbor. You shall not covet your neighbor's house. You shall not covet your neighbor's wife, or his manservant or maidservant, his ox or donkey, or anything that belongs to your neighbor.

Naismith originally develops 13 rules in the game of basketball. As the game evolved, more rules were added and modified. We should be motivated to obey rules. This governs us. In basketball, rules are made to govern us. The officials or elders are in place to make sure we obey the rules. Therefore, if we do not obey rules, we must pay a price. Spiritually, if we do not obey rules, we go to hell. In basketball, if we do not obey rules, we get a technical foul, we are out of a game, kick out, or have to pay a fine. Remember, the rules we must live by.

Soul Salvation

=

Training

"Training is like working out soul salvation."

Romans 8:28 (NIV)
And we know that in all things God works for the good of those who love him, who have been called according to his purpose.

Work for what you want. You have to pay salvation by giving your life to Christ. Salvation represents preservation. In basketball, if you do not work hard at it, you will not move up. The harder you wok, the better you become. In addition to that, the more coaches will recruit you to move up. Your work ethic is what helps preserve you in basketball. Same thing in real life, if you do not have a good work ethic, then you will lose your job or position. In order to preserve something, you must work at it. No work, no preservation. What are you doing with the time God gave you? Don't waste it.

Living Sacrifice

=

Playing the Game of Basketball

"Playing the game of basketball is like presenting yourself as a
living sacrifice."

Romans 12:1–2 (NIV)
*Therefore, I urge you, brothers, in view of God's mercy, to offer
your bodies as living sacrifices, holy and pleasing to God, this is
your spiritual act of worship. Do not conform any longer to the
pattern of this world, but be transformed by the renewing of your
mind. Then you will be able to test and approve what God's will
is his good, pleasing and perfect will.*

Every ball player must be able to sacrifice their bodies for
victory as Jesus did. Jesus died on the cross so we all have access
to experience victory. No sacrifice, no victory. Be motivated to
sacrifice yourself. If you're not ready to die for your purpose,
then chose another purpose. You must be willing to live and die
for it.

FAITH COMES BY HEARING
=
BOUNCING BASKETBALL

"Faith comes by hearing and hearing the word of God."

The basketball we now know represent the word because out of leather, something had to die in order for basketball to live. This is the same that Jesus did for us. So, in order to have faith in basketball, the basketball must continue to bounce just as the the word of God has to be continually spoken. Without it, the provision cannot be revealed. Be motivated to continue to speak Gods word. Be motivated to continue to keep the gyms open so that the basketballs can bounce so that someone can gain faith through a bouncing basketball.

SCORE TABLE

=

ALTAR

1 Kings 8:54
When Solomon had finished all these prayers and supplications to the Lord, he rose from before the altar of the Lord, where he had been kneeling with his hands spread out toward heaven.

I came up with this concept because every basketball player must kneel at the scores table before they enter the game. I chose the scores table to represent the altar because we must kneel at it before entering a game. Here is a spiritual movement that basketball players must respect and do as paying homage to the God.

CONCLUSION

This book was written in the hopes of showing people faith through basketball. Basketball is my gift and purpose in life. Never forget these concepts. These concepts will help you destroy the enemy that you face in your life. Let these illustrations help you to the fullest. Always believe when everyone else stops believing. I pray that those that read this book, will receive great empowerment and success in their life. Be blessed.

REFERENCES

Conner, Kevin J.; (1992). *Completely Revised and Expanded Interpreting The Symbols and Types*. Oregon: City Bible Publishing.

Jones, Micheal (2010). *The Basketball Dreamer of Branded Caliber Manual*. Copyrights of US Library of Congress.

Rains, Rob (2009). *The Man Who Invented Basketball*. Temple University Press

Zondervan (1996). *The Holy Bible, New International Version*. Published by Zondervan.

Micheal L. Jones is a Head Men's Basketball Coach at Pasco Hernando Community College. He is also a college Psychology Professor. He was an Athletic Director at the middle school level, in which he was awarded the Fred E. Rozelle Sportsmanship award from the Florida High School Athletic Association. Micheal Jones was inspired by his Father in basketball as a young child, where his Father snatched 36 rebounds in one game in high school. My father sacrificed his basketball career so that I could have a better life. Therefore, I chose to do the same for others by coaching. I finished playing college basketball at PHCC 1999–2001 (All-Conference). Micheal never played college basketball again. He finished his undergraduate degree at Florida State University 2004 (Track N Field 2003). Micheal has been coaching since 2005. He is now working to become AASP certified as a mental conditioning coach (Association of Applied Sports Psychology). You can follow Micheal's career at www.michealjones.net